Across GRANDMA'S GARDEN

Story by
Karen Angelucci and Lauren McDuffie

Illustrated by
Seth McDuffie

JOEY BOOKS
Morley, Missouri

Joey Books

An imprint of

Acclaim Press

Your Next Great Book

P.O. Box 238
Morley, MO 63767
(573) 262-2121
www.acclaimpress.com

Book Design: Kimberly Paul
Cover Design: Kimberly Paul
Authors: Karen Angelucci and Lauren McDuffie
Illustrator: Seth McDuffie

Library of Congress Control No.: 2012936387
ISBN-13: 978-1-935001-93-5
ISBN-10: 1-935001-93-0

First Printing: 2012
Printed in the United States of America
10 9 8 7 6 5 4 3 2 1

DEDICATIONS

To my mother, Carolyn Williams,
who continues to maintain my grandmother's garden.

Karen Angelucci

For my mother, whose unconditional love and support
have helped me grow into the person I am today.

Lauren McDuffie

With a special thank you to
an incredible author and friend, J.D. Lester.

This Book Belongs To:

____

Given By:

____

Date:

____

Across GRANDMA'S GARDEN

It's spring in
Grandma's garden,
with oh-so much to do!

Please come outside
and plant with us.
Let's go and see
what's new!

I call out to my
mother,
with boots and
trowel in hand,

"I'm going to
Grandma's
garden now!!!
We're going to
seed the land."

I whistle for Henrietta.

She knows just where I am.

Across the field to Grandma's house,
we let the screen door SLAM!

We pass some
flowering pear trees,
with petals
dewy white;

a mile of pure, green clover;
and starlings taking flight.

“Good morning, all you irises!

My favorite thing to grow!

I like the way you smell out here!
I love your purple show!”

Henri barks and
starts to dig
beneath a lilac
blossom.

Who made these tracks and nibbled here?
A bunny, bird, or 'possum?

Grandma sees us
coming,
and waves a
weathered glove.
She hollers, "Give
me sugar!"
(That's grandma-
speak for "love.")

She scoots to make
a place for me,
and gives the
ground a pat.

We'll get real good
and *dirty* here –
we're *very*
good at that!

We're wrapped up in
our garden now,
surrounded on all sides.

A damselfly just
came along
and thought she'd
take a ride!

Around us flutter
butterflies;
we hear the
buzzing bees;

we laugh at funny hummingbirds,
and smile up at the trees.

Our fingers knead the soil,
where snails and pillbugs play.
We're not afraid of worms or slugs,
they help us turn the clay!

Flowers are in
the front row,
the first to greet
the sun...

smallest next to tallest,
the rays will find each one.

Daisies wake
from winter's rest,
and Grandma
loves the cheer

of dandelions growing wild,
like *sunshine* every year!

Row by row, we sow our seeds,
with names likes *Merry Gold*.

Then magic happens underground,
with roots soon taking hold!

Grandma says we're like the plants -
some shy, and some are bold.

And me? I'm *growing like a weed!!*
At least that's what I'm told.

I hope you liked our garden.
I saved some seeds for you.
Just find a sunny spot outside,
and you'll grow magic, too!

The End.

About the Authors:

Karen Angelucci, born and raised near her grandparent's family farm in Cynthiana, Kentucky, learned early on to appreciate our connection to the environment. Her childhood, full of outdoor exploration and hard work, has inspired her to write gardening books for adults and children. Karen lives in Lexington and has two daughters, Sarah and Rachel.

Lauren McDuffie is a cookbook author and full-time writer and had the pleasure of working with Karen to bring her childhood memories to life through the words in this story. Lauren lives in Indianapolis, Indiana with her husband, Lucas.

About the Illustrator:

Seth McDuffie, a 2012 graduate of Blacksburg High School, in Blacksburg, Virginia, plans to pursue art and design in college. Having attended the exclusive Virginia Governor's School for the Visual and Performing arts, he has studied many mediums such as pottery, watercolor, oil and mixed media. Seth's hobbies, other than art, include playing the piano, singing and working at a local fine art and architecture supply store.